# Ten Poems about Herbs

Candlestick Press

Published by:
Candlestick Press,
Diversity House, 72 Nottingham Road, Arnold, Nottingham NG5 6LF, UK
www.candlestickpress.co.uk

Design and typesetting by Craig Twigg

Printed by Bayliss Printing Company Ltd of Worksop, UK

Selection and Introduction © Di Slaney, 2025

Cover illustration © Sara Boccaccini Meadows, 2025
https://www.boccaccinimeadows.com

Candlestick Press monogram © Barbara Shaw, 2008

© Candlestick Press, 2025

ISBN 978 1 913627 53 9

**Acknowledgements**

The poems in this pamphlet are reprinted from the following books, all by permission of the publishers listed unless stated otherwise. Every effort has been made to trace the copyright holders of the poems published in this book. The editor and publisher apologise if any material has been included without permission, or without the appropriate acknowledgement, and would be glad to be told of anyone who has not been consulted.

Thanks are due to all the copyright holders cited below for their kind permission.

Maggie Anderson, 'Nap Dreams' from *Cold Comfort* by Maggie Anderson © 1986. Reprinted by permission of the University of Pittsburgh Press. Sujata Bhatt, *The Stinking Rose* (Carcanet Press, 1995). Jane Burn, poem first appeared in this anthology. Jim Daniels, *Blessing the House* (University of Pittsburgh Press, 1997) © 1997 Jim Daniels, by permission of the publisher. Isobel Dixon, *A Whistling of Birds* (Nine Arches Press, 2023). John Fuller, *New Selected Poems: 1983-2008* (Chatto & Windus, 2012) by permission of United Agents. Lyn Lifshin, *Cold Comfort: Selected Poems 1970-1996* (Black Sparrow Press, 1997). Copyright © 1997 by Lyn Lifshin. Reprinted with the permission of The Permissions Company, LLC on behalf of Black Sparrow / David R Godine, Publisher, Inc., www.godine.com. Alfred Noyes, *Collected Poems* (Forgotten Books, 2020). Gibbons Ruark, *Keeping Company* (Johns Hopkins University Press, 1983) by kind permission of the author. Robert Seatter, *On the Beach with Chet Baker* (Seren Books, 2006).

All permissions cleared courtesy of Dr Suzanne Fairless-Aitken –
Swift Permissions swiftpermissions@gmail.com.

Where poets are no longer living, their dates are given.

# Contents

| | | Page |
|---|---|---|
| Introduction | *Di Slaney* | *5* |
| Basil | *Gibbons Ruark* | *7* |
| Nap Dreams | *Maggie Anderson* | *8* |
| Wild Thyme | *Lyn Lifshin* | *9* |
| Fennel | *Jim Daniels* | *10 - 11* |
| Lavender | *Alfred Noyes* | *12 - 13* |
| A Touch of Coriander | *Sujata Bhatt* | *14* |
| The Forest Knows | *Jane Burn* | *15* |
| Viper's Bugloss | *Isobel Dixon* | *16 - 17* |
| Marjoram | *John Fuller* | *18* |
| Mint | *Robert Seatter* | *19* |

## Introduction

Planting a herb garden can often be our first experience of having a garden, and sometimes it's the only garden we're able to have because of limited space. But what a garden! Within the herb family are many beautiful plants, widely varied in colour and shape and smell. Simply seeding, watering and harvesting our herbs can make us feel we are 'proper' gardeners, with the added enjoyment of all the culinary and health benefits they have to offer.

Herbs are a delight to the nose and palate, and this short selection of poems – a kitchen window box of poems, as it were – captures their heady aromas as well as their fulsome flavours. From the seductive scent of wild thyme in Lyn Lifshin's instructions of when and how best to pick "the sweet lace", to the "licorice prayer" of fennel evoking Jim Daniels' old girlfriend, these poems conjure sublime fragrances that do more than make our tastebuds tingle. They remind us of love and family, holidays and sunny days, how nature often has the answer to grief and loss. Jane Burn finds solace and healing in a forest of wild garlic, while Robert Seatter says goodbye to love while chopping the last mint of summer.

Versatile, surprising, persistent – like the very best poems, herbs don't have to take up much space to do good work. I hope these ten lovely herb poems plant themselves in some little spaces of your life and enrich them with their dreams.

*Di Slaney*

**Basil**

There in Fiesole it was always fresh
In the laneway where the spry grandfather
Tipped you his smile in the earliest wash
Of sunlight, piling strawberries high and higher
In a fragile pyramid of edible air.
Light down the years, the same sun rinses your dark
Hair over and over with brightness where
You kneel to stir the earth among thyme and chard,
Rosemary and the gathering of mints,
The rough leaf picked for tea this summer noon,
The smooth one saved for *pesto* in the winter,
For the cold will come, though you turn to me soon,
Your eyes going serious green from hazel,
Your quick hand on my face the scent of basil.


*Gibbons Ruark*

**Nap Dreams**

Tarragon, basil, parsley, dill, the noisy smells
at the front of the garden by the marigolds never
sleep long. Their dreams are only a brief reprieve
from aroma. They drowse among the warm bees
and grow into condiments. The purple basil
has tiny sauce dreams; the tarragon dreams
chicken. The parsley dreams potato's little
sister, the pillowslip's green crewel. The dill
hovers over all the rows and drifts yellow seeds
onto cucumbers it schemes to marry, to gain
citizenship in the alien country of solid food.
Rarely do the herbs remember their dreams, their
swift, upright lapses of industry.


*Maggie Anderson*

## Wild Thyme

all the way down the
sloped hill under
the white pines
You should pick it when
the sun is low and night's
water is wild on the
red grass. Don't kick up
the sweet lace, twist
or crunch out the smell
But pick it while it's
sucking up afternoon
light, its smell on
your fingers like
a lover, pin it to
beams in rooms apricot
light will sneak thru
glazing bare walnuts,
knowing the leaves
still wait in snow
full of what drew
you to it


*Lyn Lifshin (1942 – 2019)*

# Fennel

grows behind the house
among wildflowers and plain weeds—
soothing green, licorice sweet,
sweet as the child bundled up
kicking stones down the street.

Ah, wild fennel wet in the morning—
your delicate sprigs
the hair of an old girlfriend.

I am bundled up these days, long hours
of silent work, corkscrewing in.
Bumping off stone walls, I fill myself
with the pebble of each thought.
Gravel shifts inside me, blood
thick as wet cement.

My neck stiffens from turning pages,
the downward slant. Church bells
across the dirt road clang against
clappers. I try to imagine the intimacy
of hands pulling ropes. The automatic ringing
mocks me on the hour.

Last night I watched car lights wind
through the hills, crazy stars.
Against black night, what do I have to say?

It's time to go in and toss another log
in the stove. My knees are damp with dew
but I wanted you to know
I've been thinking of you.

Look, the fog is lifting its thick cough,
the sun is pushing its yellow hand through.
I close my eyes and inhale
your licorice prayer.

Wild fennel, my sweet little telephone,
I haven't spoken to anyone in days
and I am speaking to you.


*Jim Daniels*

## Lavender

Lavender, lavender,
   That makes your linen sweet;
The hawker brings his basket
   Down the sooty street:
The dirty doors and pavements
   Are simmering in the heat:
He brings a dream to London,
   And drags his weary feet.

Lavender, lavender,
   From where the bee hums,
To the loud roar of London,
   With purple dreams he comes,
From raggéd lanes of wild-flowers
   To raggéd London slums,
With a basket full of lavender
   And purple dreams he comes.

Is it nought to you that hear him?
   With the old strange cry
The weary hawker passes,
   And some will come and buy,
And some will let him pass away
   And only heave a sigh,
But most will neither heed nor hear
   When dreams go by.

*Lavender, lavender!*
   *His songs were fair and sweet,*
*He brought us harvests out of heaven,*
   *Full sheaves of radiant wheat;*
*He brought us keys to Paradise,*
   *And hawked them thro' the street;*
*He brought his dreams to London,*
   *And dragged his weary feet.*

Lavender, lavender!
   He is gone. The sunset glows;
But through the brain of London
   The mystic fragrance flows.
Each foggy cell remembers,
   Each raggéd alley knows,
The land he left behind him,
   The land to which he goes.


*Alfred Noyes (1880 – 1958)*

## A Touch of Coriander

*Garlic is believed to act as an aphrodisiac*
*when pounded with fresh coriander*
*and taken with neat wine.*
     -     Gaius Pliny the Elder

It is the coriander – the green leaves
that cool the tongue
after garlic. It is the coriander: feathery, tender,
that makes them undress each other
before they've finished undressing the garlic –

And the wine? With garlic
the wine only makes them thirstier –
the wine only makes the kiss last longer.

And then they'll turn
again to coriander – the green leaves
that soothe the eyelids.


*Sujata Bhatt*

## The Forest Knows

I will stand still, and I will breathe –
quietly, as if I do not want to be discovered.
I will breathe deeply, slowly
and navigate this intricate web of smells –
inhale the bodies of wood, the new growth,
the rich depth of leaf-mould,
the subtle mosses that bloom from ground and bark,
like mysteries. I walk on,
until a plush of wild garlic ripples around my feet.
The white globe-shaped flowers grow here
like a private universe –
their green leaves beckon in the breeze.
Their scent is made from every meal
I wish, right now, I could eat. I pluck a stem
and test its flavour upon my tongue.
Herb of courage, healing herb, herb of protection,
no folklore spirit can claim me now.
I will stand so still and quietly here
because I am not alone.
Around me is language – the elusive speech
of precious trees transferring, leaf to leaf;
threading, root to root.
The air here echoes with ancient voice
and I am here to listen.
Above me, each incredible crown
whispers against the endless sky.
I am only small against this realm.
The forest knows that I am not afraid.


*Jane Burn*

## Viper's Bugloss

*"a most gallant herb of the sun"*

Flaring up with its pilot flame blue
like nothing I have ever seen,
blue as the rare blue sky of June,
Midsummer Common hot as its name.

*"Blueweed, Snakeflower, Viper's Grass"*

The herb-seller's reeling these off,
but I'm testing the words from the tag
on my tongue: strange bugle, floral
glossolalias, the trumpets serpentine.

*"a most singular remedy against poyson"*

with its stalks all speckled like snakes,
its adder-fashioned seeds. But who needs muti
for a scorpion's sting in Cambridgeshire?
Cures for unlikely things, charlatan's dream

*"it will bring you bees and butterflies"*

she says, bagging mint and rosemary
for me. Its fortressed spines against
the ants, those useless pollen pilferers,
but bees can scrounge, a larval feast.

*"abundance of milk in women's breasts"*

procured, Culpeper says, by the seed
drunk soaked in wine. Which eases pain,
also, in the kidneys, back and loins.
Sine qua non: milk, honey, poor man's opium.

*"passions and tremblings of the heart"*

But too much honey can prove fatal.
Vicious March, a dumbstruck April
and the weeks I'd sleepwalked since.
I needed something beautiful to grow.

*"swooning, sadness, melancholy"*

This was the year I learned the art
of weeping secretly, though in full view.
Trains, theatres, or Strawberry Fair –
the trick, the sleight-of-heart's the same.

*"it grows best in the dry and the waste"*

I ripped the mint out later, greedy spreader,
but the rosemary burgeons, on and on.
My newfound simple lit the garden
with its blue of loss a while, was gone.

Perhaps it is the way of grief's abatement
that I cannot mark a calendar with when.


*Isobel Dixon*

## Marjoram

I might have cut the marjoram for salad,
And did so, until the rainy days drove
Me indoors, and it was all forgotten.

Their little spears of green, with over-notes
Of rust or leather, are now emerald pillars
Supporting tiny clusters of pink flowers.

I counted seventeen bees upon them, delicately
Rampaging (seventeen until I could reliably
Count no more, as they circled and changed places).

I shall, I think, straddle the back of one of them,
Gripping its tigery fur, and fly away
To see where they make their honey, and to taste it.

*John Fuller*

**Mint**

I am chopping up the last mint of summer.
It's a ritual goodbye –

goes with sandals, bare legs, shorts, and suntan lotion,
alfresco dinners and the candles burning
to a waxed stump
among the garden leaves.

Last mint on my fingers now,
the scent of it pushed through my hair
when I lift my hand
from a finishing touch to dinner.

Last ritual in a ritual,
and everything I've ever learned
seems to come back
to the comfort and confines of cycles such as these –

how I am balanced on the last, sharp edges
of that pepper scent which I want to be everywhere,
holding it close
with every intensity I shall ever have,

and how I forget it, in the snow-filled silence
of my three-month-hence garden,
so I wonder to myself

Did I ever eat mint? Did I ever crush it on the circle
of this wide blue plate? Did I ever crave a summer,
long and green and full of this?

The mystery is
what we do with loves even as small as this –
how we learn to live with them,
how we learn to forget.

*Robert Seatter*